"YOU'D BUTTER BELIEVE THIS IS THE ONLY BAKING BOOK YOU'LL NEED"

D0810467

**BAKING—
IT'S A PIECE
OF CAKE**

Warning: this book may contain traces of puns.

RUNNING PRESS
PHILADELPHIA

PHOTOGRAPHY BY LUISA BRIMBLE

ILLUSTRATIONS BY ALICE OEHR

Good Things Come to Those Who Bake

Charlotte Ree

JUST DESSERTS

CONTENTS

DEDICAKETION

This book is dedicated to anyone who says they can't bake. Trust me that you can, and with this little book, I hope that you will.

I get such a great deal of pleasure from the process of baking. I discovered a love for it as a way to not only nail my sweet cravings, but to unwind after a busy working week. There is something truly wonderful about taking the time to stop and focus, put your phone away and get swept up in a recipe.

I am a no-fuss baker, and good, delicious, mouth-watering recipes really do not have to be complicated. My recipes are easy and made to taste amazing more than just look pretty. This book aims to fill your baking arsenal with simple, tried-and-tested, trustworthy staples that you can bake day in, day out, to please even the pickiest of eaters. I hope it will build your confidence and show you just how simple it can be to create amazing desserts.

I am not just baking to eat, I'm really baking so that I can share the results with someone. There are many recipes in this book that take no more than 30 minutes to put together, and the joy and sheer satisfaction you feel when gifting a classic, simple, easy-to-bake cake to someone will encourage you to bake more, and will have people knocking at your door.

> **66** *I HOPE THIS LITTLE BOOK WILL BECOME YOUR SIDECAKE IN THE KITCHEN* **99**

The other things you must know before embarking on this little journey are my non-negotiables when it comes to baking:

Read through a new recipe in its entirety before you begin, to make sure you have all of the ingredients and equipment and have allocated the time needed. Baking is a science, so you will want to follow the method to the tee to ensure you end up with a cake that is risen, moist and delicious.

INTRODUCTION

Remember that no two ovens are the same. All recipes in this book have been tested in my oven at home, a standard domestic oven using the conventional baking setting. It may be worthwhile getting your hands on an oven thermometer to check your oven temperature—you can also use it to check for hot spots to avoid burning your cakes.

My beautiful friend Nadine Ingram taught me that the most important rule of thumb when it comes to baking is to **follow your intuition,** and there is no better time to do this than when it comes to your oven. Use the cooking time for each recipe as a guide only, with the view to check on what you're baking about 10–15 minutes before the stated finish time. If you are baking cookies or layer cakes, you will want to swap/turn the trays halfway through to ensure they bake evenly. When checking or turning your cakes, be sure to open your oven for the least amount of time possible to prevent heat loss.

Use a bamboo or wooden skewer (avoid metal, as it is slippery) to test your cakes. Insert it into the middle of the cake—if it comes out clean, then the cake is cooked. If you notice that your cake is cooking too quickly on top and not all the way through, you can cover the top of it with heavy-duty aluminum foil to prevent it from burning.

A stand mixer is your best investment as a baker—I simply could not live without mine. The benefit is that you don't need to be beating, creaming, folding or whisking, as the mixer does it for you. Instead, you can use that time as I do—to wash dishes, tidy the kitchen and prepare for the next steps of your recipe. It also means you are more likely to bake, as the process isn't so time-consuming. Most recipes in this book require you to use the whisk attachment of your stand mixer.

If you are only just beginning to dabble in baking and don't want to make the commitment to a stand mixer just yet, simply use hand-held electric beaters. They are small, convenient, inexpensive and easily transportable. I often take mine on holidays with me.

Some of the recipes in this book don't require a stand or electric mixer, and **you can simply use a mixing bowl and whisk or wooden spoon.** It's always handy to have a variety of different-sized bowls. Stainless steel bowls are nonreactive and heatproof and are my preference. You can also use them in lieu of a double boiler to melt chocolate.

You'll notice that all of my ingredients are measured in grams. This is because I use an electric scale, which, apart from my stand mixer, is the most important piece of equipment in my kitchen. It is so much more accurate, and there's nothing more important than being precise with measurements when baking. The best part is that you can place a mixing bowl on the scale and set it to tare before you add each ingredient, allowing you to measure various ingredients of differing weights one after the other in the same bowl. Life-changing.

I use standard **US measuring cups and spoons** in all of the recipes in this book. If you do choose to use cups and spoons instead of a digital scale, you will want to shake the ingredient loosely into the cup; don't pack it in. Level off the surface with the blade of a knife or a metal spatula.

INGREDIENTS

All of the ingredients used in this book are easily found at your local grocery store. There are some optional decorative items, such as edible flowers, edible gold dust or freeze-dried raspberries, that may be a little trickier to find, but specialty stores online stock all of these, and much more.

Baking with ingredients at room temperature makes a huge difference in the final result. If you forgot to leave your butter out to soften, you can either cut it into cubes or use a grater to speed up the softening process.

You'll want to get into the habit of breaking your eggs into a small bowl before adding to the cake batter to avoid egg shells or one bad egg ruining the cake entirely. It's the same for making pavlova—separate your egg whites and yolks in small bowls individually to ensure you don't mix the two accidentally. Large, free-range eggs (approximately 2 ounces/60 g each) were used for all the recipes in this book.

Given that my recipes are simple and pared back, you will want to purchase the best-quality ingredients that you can afford to really allow the flavors to shine. Good chocolate, in particular, is crucial to the desserts you make. I use top-quality, dark cooking chocolate with 70% cocoa solids and Dutch-processed cocoa powder for a moist, fudgy and rich chocolate flavor.

EQUIPMENT

Regarding bakeware, you can slowly add to your collection over time, starting out with the essentials—a classic springform pan, Bundt pan, rectangular baking sheet and loaf pan. You can then work your way up from there, just like I have, to amass a diverse collection of bakeware that will have you covered for desserts of all shapes and sizes.

GREASING THE PANS

Before you begin baking, ensure that you have greased and lined your cake pans or baking sheets, have your oven racks in the correct position and have preheated your oven to the specified temperature.

When it comes to greasing your pans, it doesn't have to be time-consuming or difficult. For springform pans, simply cut a square of parchment paper that is 2 inches/5 cm bigger

than your pan on each side and place on the base of the pan; then get the ring of the pan and place it tightly over the base so there are no wrinkles in the parchment paper. Close the spring tightly and lock it into place. Generously spray the inside of the ring with nonstick cooking spray (I use canola oil spray). For rectangular, square, madeleine, muffin or friand pans, I use the spray only. Bundt cakes can get a little trickier, so here's a little bit about Bundt pans specifically . . .

THE THING ABOUT BUNDTS

I adore them. A Bundt pan is a magical cake pan that looks more like a piece of art than your regular bakeware. Bundt pans come in all shapes and sizes; you can, of course, make any of my Bundt cakes in an 8-inch/20-cm springform pan instead, though they won't be as visually striking. You can find some extraordinary Bundt pans online. These pans are nonstick, distribute heat quickly and bake evenly.

The trick here is that you need to grease your pan generously. You can use a pastry brush and softened (room temperature) butter to grease your Bundt pans, then lightly sprinkle with flour, tipping out any excess before filling with batter.

You can also use a nonstick cooking spray, such as canola spray, which is incredibly effective and my preferred method. For the more intricate pan designs, I recommend doubling up and using both techniques.

Also, and most importantly, allow your Bundt cake to cool completely in the pan before turning it out. You won't get anywhere by being impatient. I always say a little prayer to the baking gods and give the pan a gentle tap all over before lifting the pan away from the cake.

For me, the most beautiful thing about baking a Bundt is seeing the face of the person you gift it to—utter delight!

THE FOLLOWING CAKE PANS ARE USED IN THIS BOOK, BUT PLEASE DON'T STRESS IF YOU'RE MISSING ANY—MY RECIPES ARE VERY FLEXIBLE:

9-inch or 8-inch (23 cm or 20 cm) springform pan

13 x 9 x 2½-inch (33 x 23 x 6 cm) rectangular baking sheet

16 capacity madeleine pan

12-cup friand pan

9 x 5 x 3-inch (23 x 13 x 7 cm) loaf pan

12-cup muffin pan

Classic Bundt pan

8 x 2-inch (20 x 5 cm) square pan

2 rectangular baking sheets

15 x 10 x 1-inch (38 x 25 x 3 cm) jelly roll pan

9 x 4-inch (23 x 10 cm) angel food cake pan (preferably with feet)

12 x 8 x 1¼-inch (30 x 20 x 3.5 cm) sheet pan

ADDITIONAL ITEMS THAT ARE INCREDIBLY USEFUL TO HAVE IN YOUR BAKING KIT:

Pastry brush

"SIEVE THE DAY"

Balloon whisk

Heat-resistant spatula, to stir hot ingredients or scrape down bowls

Palette knife for frosting cakes (also handy for sliding under cakes and cookies to transfer from their trays to wire cooling racks)

Measuring cup, either plastic or glass, to measure liquids

Food processor to chop nuts or blitz cookies into a crumb (this is a non-essential appliance, but it can make your life easier and the baking process quicker for certain recipes)

Small metal sieve to dust and decorate desserts

Large metal spoon, to fold ingredients such as meringue together

Large metal sieve to sift ingredients like cocoa powder and confectioners' sugar

COOKIES, BARS & SWEETS

NUTELLA THUMBPRINT COOKIES

Chocolate, hazelnut and sea salt may just be three of my favorite flavors, and they unite in the form of my Nutella Thumbprint Cookies. These are so quick and easy to make—they're the perfect weekend baking project.

You will want to sit your Nutella jar in a bowl of warm water for 2–3 minutes to make the Nutella silky and smooth, allowing you to spoon it easily onto your cookies. →

"LOST WITHOUT CHEW"

MAKES 16

¾ cup (125 g) dark chocolate (70% cocoa), roughly chopped

4½ ounces (125 g) unsalted butter, at room temperature

⅓ cup (80 g) superfine sugar

1 teaspoon vanilla extract

1 large egg, at room temperature

1¼ cups (160 g) all-purpose flour, sifted

¼ cup (30 g) Dutch-processed cocoa powder, sifted

1 cup (290 g) Nutella

sea salt flakes

Melt the chocolate in a heatproof bowl over a saucepan of simmering water, or by using a double boiler. Don't allow the bowl to touch the water. Set aside to cool.

Beat the butter and sugar in the bowl of a stand mixer fitted with the whisk attachment until light and fluffy. Add the vanilla, egg and chocolate, and beat until combined. Add the flour and cocoa powder and beat until a dough forms.

Roll the cookie dough into a log, then wrap in parchment paper. Leave it in the fridge for an hour.

Preheat the oven to 325°F (160°C). Line two baking sheets with parchment paper.

Remove the dough from the fridge and form walnut-sized balls of dough with your hands. Place the balls on the prepared baking sheets, leaving a 2-inch (5 cm) gap between each to allow for spreading. Use your thumb to press an indentation into the center of each ball.

Bake for 13–15 minutes, or until dried and slightly cracked. Allow to cool slightly on the baking sheets before transferring to a cooling rack to cool completely. (While the cookies are still hot, you can use your thumb to press them further if the indentation has been lost in the baking process.)

Once cooled, spoon a little Nutella into the center of each cookie and sprinkle with sea salt. Store leftovers in an airtight container at room temperature for up to a week.

TIP: *We used black sea salt flakes here for a fabulous contrast with the Nutella.*

"DON'T GO BAKING MY HEART"

SHORTBREAD
JELLY HEARTS

I can't beat sugar, butter, and vanilla together without scooping up
a bit to try. With the very first taste, I am immediately transported back
to my nanny's kitchen, licking the same mixture from a spatula
as we made jelly drops together.

These are incredibly easy to make, and they can be customized to include
your favorite flavor of jelly. Here I have chosen raspberry, as that's my
nanny's favorite and the jelly we always baked with, but you could use
fig, blueberry, strawberry or anything that tickles your fancy, really.
Just be careful not to overfill or the jelly may ooze out. →

MAKES 12

2 sticks (225 g) unsalted butter, at room temperature

¾ cup (170 g) superfine sugar

2 large egg yolks, at room temperature

1 teaspoon vanilla extract

1 cup (100 g) almond meal

2 cups (250 g) all-purpose flour

½ teaspoon sea salt

½ teaspoon ground cinnamon

1 teaspoon finely grated lemon zest

¼ cup (30 g) confectioners' sugar, sifted

½ cup (160 g) raspberry jelly

TIP: You can skip the heart shapes altogether if you want—just sandwich the jelly between two solid cookies instead.

In the bowl of a stand mixer fitted with the whisk attachment, cream the butter and superfine sugar together until light and fluffy (about 2 minutes). Add the egg yolks and beat for 1 minute, then add the vanilla.

In a large mixing bowl, combine the almond meal, flour, salt, cinnamon and lemon zest.

Add the dry ingredients to the butter mixture and beat lightly to combine.

Divide the dough in half and gently press each half into a disk. Wrap the disks in plastic wrap and refrigerate for at least 30 minutes.

Preheat the oven to 350°F (170°C). Line two baking sheets with parchment paper.

Remove the dough from the fridge. On a lightly floured surface, roll out the dough to a thickness of ¼ inch (6 mm). If your dough sticks, keep dusting it with more flour and rolling until it is no longer sticking to your hands. If it softens too much, put it back in the fridge for a little while to firm up.

Using a 2¾-inch (7 cm) circular cutter, cut out as many cookies as you can manage from the disk of dough. Keep re-rolling the dough until you run out. Repeat with the second disk of dough, but this time after you have cut out your circles, use a 2 inch (5 cm) heart-shaped cutter to cut hearts from the center of each. Use a palette knife to assist you with picking up the cut-outs, being gentle to stop them from breaking. You can use the leftover dough from cutting out the hearts to make additional cookies.

Bake the cookies for 12 minutes, or until lightly golden-brown on the edges—you may need to swap the trays halfway through to ensure the cookies bake evenly.

Remove the cookies from the oven and, using a spatula, carefully transfer them to a cooling rack.

When ready to assemble, dust confectioners' sugar over the tops of the cut-out circles only.

Using a small teaspoon, spread jelly over each of the solid circles. Top each one with a dusted cookie and serve. Store leftovers in an airtight container at room temperature for up to a week.

CHOCOLATE AMARETTI

My Grandma and Papa took me to Italy when I was 13, and so began my love affair with all things Italian. I have since learned the language, traveled all over the country, and I live and breathe Italian food. Amaretti cookies are one of my favorite Italian desserts. They are incredibly simple to make and so delicious—six ingredients and 15 minutes in the oven are all it takes.

**AMARETTI?
YOU BET I AM!**

MAKES 16

2 large egg whites, at room temperature

½ teaspoon almond extract

2 cups (200 g) almond meal

½ cup (50 g) Dutch-processed cocoa powder, sifted

¼ teaspoon sea salt

1 cup (125 g) confectioners' sugar, sifted, plus extra for rolling

Preheat the oven to 325°F (160°C). Line a large baking sheet with parchment paper.

Whisk the egg whites in a bowl until frothy but not yet white. Add the almond extract and whisk to combine.

Place the almond meal, cocoa powder, salt and confectioners' sugar in a large bowl and make a well in the center. Add the egg whites and mix together to form a stiff dough.

Before rolling the balls, dust the palms of your hands with a little confectioners' sugar—this will prevent the mixture from sticking to your hands. Roll the mixture into walnut-sized balls, then roll each ball in confectioners' sugar. Place on the prepared baking sheet, spaced 1¼ inch (3 cm) apart. Bake for 15 minutes, or until the cookies are lightly golden and cracked on top. Cool on the baking sheet for 5 minutes before transferring to a wire rack to cool completely. These cookies can be stored in an airtight container at room temperature for up to a week.

TIP: If you would like to make traditional almond amaretti, simply replace the cocoa powder in this recipe with confectioners' sugar.

A NOD TO THE KING OF COOKIES

The first bite of a Kingston immediately transports me back to my Australian childhood. They were the best cookies in the Arnott's 'Assorted Creams' pack and always the first to be devoured. My brother and I would visit my nanny every school holiday, and we would race each other to the pantry, hoping to be the first and to claim our beloved cookies.

The only thing better than a Kingston fresh from the pack is a homemade one. The oaty, golden syrup cookie could easily disguise itself as an Australian Anzac cookie but is transformed when combined with silky milk chocolate. With ingredients that are most likely already in your pantry, it is a recipe that you will return to time and time again.

66 *A BATCH MADE IN HEAVEN* 99

MAKES 12

1⅓ cups (165 g) all-purpose flour

1 teaspoon baking soda

5½ ounces (150 g) unsalted
butter, at room temperature

½ cup (120 g) turbinado sugar

¼ cup (80 g) golden syrup

¾ cup (80 g) desiccated coconut

¾ cup (80 g) rolled oats

1⅓ cups (200 g) milk chocolate,
roughly chopped

Preheat the oven to 325°F (160°C). Line two baking sheets with parchment paper. Sift the flour and baking soda together.

In the bowl of a stand mixer fitted with the whisk attachment, cream the butter, sugar and golden syrup until pale and fluffy. Add the flour, baking soda, coconut and rolled oats and mix until combined.

Roll teaspoons (about ¾ ounce or 20 g) of the mixture into balls and place on the prepared trays, spaced 1¼ inches (3 cm) apart. Flatten slightly with the palm of your hand. Bake for 15 minutes, or until golden.

Remove the baking sheets from the oven and transfer the cookies to a cooling rack to cool completely.

Melt the chocolate in a heatproof bowl over a saucepan of simmering water, or by using a double boiler. Don't allow the bowl to touch the water.

Leave to cool slightly, and when the chocolate has thickened, spread over the base of half the cookies. Sandwich with the remaining cookies and serve. Store leftovers in an airtight container at room temperature for up to a week.

" YOU'RE ONE IN A DOZEN "

HONEY MADELEINES

Madeleines—the little French butter cakes that stole my heart. This is as close to teleportation as it gets for me—with one bite of these, I am whisked away to Paris. Here's my take on a beautiful classic. Easy to whip up, you'll be devouring them within 20 minutes. →

"WON'T YOU BEE MY MADELEINE?"

MAKES 16

4½ ounces (125 g) unsalted butter

¼ cup (60 ml) honey

2 large eggs, at room temperature

¼ cup (50 g) superfine sugar

¾ cup (100 g) all-purpose flour, sifted

1 teaspoon baking powder, sifted

confectioners' sugar, sifted, for dusting

heavy whipping cream, whipped, to serve (optional)

Preheat the oven to 350°F (170°C). Grease 16 holes of a madeleine pan with nonstick cooking spray.

Melt the butter in a saucepan and remove from the heat. Stir in the honey and allow to cool.

In the bowl of a stand mixer fitted with the whisk attachment, whisk the eggs and sugar until pale and fluffy. Add the flour, baking powder and honey mixture and fold together.

Pour the mixture into the prepared madeleine pan, leaving an ⅛ inch (3 mm) gap from the top of each hole. Bake for 10 minutes until golden. Cool on a cooling rack. Serve dusted with confectioners' sugar and with some heavy whipping cream on the side, if you like. Alternatively, eat them warm straight from the pan, just like we did on the shoot. These are best eaten on the day they're made.

"HONEY, I'M COMB"

SHORTBREAD
CARAMEL BAR

❝ RAISE THE BAR ❞

For the longest time, Hetty McKinnon's salted caramel bar was the only caramel bar I would bake. Hers is made with a crunchy cookie base, similar to an Australian Anzac cookie, and remains to this day my ultimate indulgence. This is my own recipe, but with a twist. Using a shortbread cookie base, the bar is then topped with thick salted caramel and rich dark chocolate (and some caramel popcorn, but you can skip this bit if you like). I am a salt fiend, so if you would prefer yours less salty, simply use unsalted butter. →

SERVES 18

1¾ cups (225 g) all-purpose flour, sifted

⅔ cup (115 g) rice flour, sifted

⅔ cup (120 g) superfine sugar

pinch of sea salt

7 ounces (200 g) salted butter, at room temperature

TOPPING

5½ ounces (150 g) salted butter

¾ cup (150 g) superfine sugar

⅓ cup (80 ml) golden syrup

1¼ cups (400 g) sweetened condensed milk

½ teaspoon sea salt, or more if you are a salt fiend like me

1⅓ cups (200 g) dark chocolate (70% cocoa), roughly chopped

Preheat the oven to 300°F (150°C). Grease and line a 12 x 8 x 1¼-inch (30 x 20 x 3.5 cm) sheet pan with parchment paper.

Combine the flours, sugar and salt in a bowl. Rub the butter in with your fingers until a crumble begins to form. Place in the pan and flatten out evenly with the back of a wooden spoon. Bake in the oven for 40 minutes, or until golden. Remove from the oven and prick the shortbread with a fork. Allow to cool completely in the pan.

To make the topping, place the butter, sugar, golden syrup, condensed milk and salt in a wide, heavy-based saucepan and heat gently, stirring to melt the butter. Bring to a simmer and continue to simmer for about 10–15 minutes, stirring constantly to stop the mixture sticking to the bottom of the pan and burning. When the caramel is thick and fudgy, pour it over the shortbread and smooth out with a palette knife. Leave to set for 30 minutes.

Melt the chocolate in a double boiler, or in a heatproof bowl set over a saucepan of simmering water (ensuring the bowl doesn't touch the water). When melted, spread it evenly over the set caramel. Leave for 2 hours to set, then turn out and cut into 18 pieces. Store in an airtight container in the fridge for up to a week.

“ *FEW AND BAR BETWEEN* ”

CHOCOLATE-CHIP ICE-CREAM SANDWICHES

Someone once asked me what vessel I wanted
my ice cream to be served in. My answer? The tub. The only
thing better than eating ice cream straight from the tub is
eating it wedged between my chocolate-chip cookies.
Chewy chocolate and ice cream, the ultimate indulgence. →

MAKES 12 SANDWICHES

9 ounces (250 g) salted butter, at room temperature, divided

¾ cup (160 g) light brown sugar

2 teaspoons vanilla extract

½ cup (115 g) turbinado sugar

1 large egg, at room temperature

2⅓ cups (300 g) all-purpose flour

1 teaspoon baking soda

1 cup (160 g) milk chocolate chips

1 pint of good-quality neapolitan or vanilla bean ice cream

Place 4½ ounces (125 g) of the butter in a small saucepan and brown over medium heat until amber in color, stirring occasionally. Ensure that you keep an eye on the pan as it only takes a few seconds to burn the butter. Once browned, pour the butter into a small bowl and leave to cool.

Using a stand mixer fitted with the whisk attachment, cream the remaining butter and the brown sugar until light and fluffy. Add the vanilla, browned butter, sugar and egg, and mix until combined.

Sift the flour and baking soda into the bowl and mix until combined. Scrape down the side of the bowl and fold in the chocolate chips. Wrap the cookie dough in plastic wrap and roll into a log. Leave in the fridge for an hour.

Preheat the oven to 350 °F (170°C). Line a baking sheet with parchment paper.

Roll the dough into walnut-sized balls and place on the prepared baking sheet , leaving a 2-inch (5 cm) gap between each cookie to allow for spreading. If you want to be precise, I roll my dough into 1 ounce (25 g) balls.

Flatten the cookies slightly using your hand. Bake for 13 minutes, or until golden. Remove from the oven and allow to cool.

Remove the ice cream from the freezer and allow to thaw for 5 minutes so it is easier to scoop. Arrange the cookies on a cooling rack, pairing the cookies according to their size. To serve, place scoops of ice cream between the cookies and sandwich together. Eat immediately, or wrap them in plastic wrap and freeze for later. They're best eaten within 2-3 days—if frozen, allow them to soften slightly before serving.

" MY HEART
MELTS FOR YOU "

BROWN BUTTER
& SALTED CARAMEL
COOKIES

My friend Amelia first introduced me to the joys of brown butter,
and once I had tried it there was no going back. Brown butter adds
a rich, nutty taste to these cookies and creates the most
wonderful aroma in your kitchen. →

I LOVE YOU DOUGH MUCH

MAKES 24

9 ounces (250 g) salted butter, at room temperature, divided

¾ cup (160 g) dark brown sugar

2 teaspoons vanilla extract

½ cup (115 g) turbinado sugar

1 large egg, at room temperature

3¼ cups (400 g) all-purpose flour

1 teaspoon baking soda

CARAMEL

1¼ cups (250 g) superfine sugar

2 teaspoons sea salt

Brown 4½ ounces (125 g) of the butter in a small saucepan over medium heat until amber in color, stirring occasionally. Ensure that you keep an eye on the pan as it only takes a few seconds to burn the butter. Once browned, pour the butter into a bowl and leave to cool.

While your butter cools, make the caramel. Line a baking sheet with a silicone mat or parchment paper. Place the superfine sugar and salt in a medium saucepan over medium heat. Heat the sugar until it melts, whisking constantly to avoid burning. Cook until amber in color and smoking—if you don't see smoke then the caramel won't have any flavor. Pour onto the prepared baking sheet and set aside to cool.

For the dough, cream the remaining butter and the brown sugar in the bowl of a stand mixer fitted with the whisk attachment until light and fluffy. Add the vanilla, browned butter, turbinado sugar and egg, and mix until combined.

Sift the flour and baking soda into the bowl and mix until combined. Scrape down the sides of the bowl.

Place a clean dish towel over the cooled caramel and hit gently with a rolling pin to break it into bite-sized pieces (note that the caramel shards will be sharp, but they'll soften in the oven), then carefully fold it into the dough. Wrap the cookie dough in plastic wrap and roll into a log. Leave in the fridge for an hour.

Preheat the oven to 350°F (170°C). Line two baking sheets with parchment paper.

Roll the dough into walnut-sized balls and place on the prepared baking sheet, leaving a 2-inch (5 cm) gap between each cookie to allow for spreading. If you want to be precise, I roll my dough into 1 ounce (25 g) balls.

Flatten the cookies slightly using your hand. Bake for 15 minutes, or until golden. Remove from the oven and leave to cool on the baking sheet. Store in an airtight container at room temperature for up to a week.

CHOCOLATE BROWNIES

66 *YOU'LL GET BROWNIE POINTS FOR BAKING THESE* 99

Brownies were one of the first things I made as a home baker, and I love them in their purest form—chocolate on chocolate! The edge pieces from the brownie pan are always my favorites because of that added crunch. You can make these brownies in a regular 12-cup muffin pan so they're crunchy all around and gooey and moist in the middle. →

MAKES 9

1¾ cups (350 g) superfine sugar

⅔ cup (80 g) Dutch-processed cocoa powder, sifted, plus extra for dusting (optional)

1¼ cups (150 g) all-purpose flour, sifted

1 teaspoon baking powder, sifted

3 large eggs, at room temperature

7 ounces (200 g) unsalted butter, melted and cooled

2 teaspoons vanilla extract

¾ cup (125 g) dark chocolate (70% cocoa), roughly chopped

ice cream, to serve (optional)

confectioners' sugar, for dusting (optional)

Preheat the oven to 325 °F (160°C). Butter or spray and line a 8 x 8 x 2-inch (20 x 5 cm) square baking pan with parchment paper.

Mix the sugar, cocoa powder, flour and baking powder in a large bowl. Add the eggs, butter and vanilla and whisk by hand until combined, then stir in the chocolate.

Pour the batter into the prepared pan and bake for 40 minutes.

Leave to cool slightly in the pan, then turn out onto a wire rack. Cut into nine pieces.

You could serve these warm in the pan with a generous dollop of ice cream or simply dust with cocoa powder or confectioners' sugar. Store leftovers in an airtight container at room temperature for up to 2 days.

APPLE HAND PIES

A sweet and comforting recipe for apple hand pies, delicious pockets of warmth. I use ready-made pie crust dough in this recipe, but you can make your own from scratch using your favorite recipe. →

"APPLEY EVER AFTER"

MAKES 12

14 ounces (400 g) Granny Smith apples (about 3), peeled, cored and cut into ¾-inch (2 cm) pieces

½ cup (100 g) superfine sugar

¼ teaspoon ground cinnamon

¼ teaspoon ground nutmeg

4 teaspoons vanilla bean paste

2 pounds (850 g) store-bought pie crust dough, thawed

1 large egg, lightly beaten

turbinado sugar, for sprinkling

vanilla ice cream, to serve

Place the apple, superfine sugar, cinnamon, nutmeg, vanilla and ⅔ cup (150 ml) of water in a saucepan and bring to the boil over medium heat. Reduce the heat to low and simmer, stirring occasionally, for a further 15–20 minutes until the apple is soft. Leave to cool.

Once the pastry is thawed, cut out 24 circles using a 3½-inch (9 cm) rounds.

Preheat the oven to 400°F (200°C). Line two baking sheets with parchment paper.

Place half the pastry rounds on the prepared trays. Top with a dollop of apple mixture, leaving a ½-inch (1 cm) border. Brush the edges of the pastry circles with the beaten egg, top with the remaining pastry rounds and seal the edges with a fork. Cut a small, shallow cross in the top of each pie with a sharp knife, then brush with beaten egg and sprinkle with turbinado sugar. Bake until golden (approximately 25 minutes), turning the baking sheets halfway to ensure even cooking.

Allow to cool for 10 minutes on a cooling rack, then serve warm with a scoop of vanilla ice cream. Cover leftovers and store in the fridge for up to 2 days.

RASPBERRY
FRIANDS

These little almond cakes are basically a classy version
of muffins. The thing that appeals most to me is that
you can have all of the benefits of a cake, in mini
individual portions. I find these are best consumed while
still warm. You will need a friand pan to make them. →

MAKES 12

6 large egg whites,
at room temperature

5½ ounces (150 g) unsalted
butter, melted and cooled

1¼ cups (125 g) almond meal

2 cups (250 g) confectioners'
sugar, sifted, plus extra for dusting

¾ cup (100 g) all-purpose flour,
sifted

1 cup (125 g) fresh or frozen
raspberries

Preheat the oven to 325°F (160°C). Lightly grease a
12-cup friand pan with nonstick cooking spray.

Whisk the egg whites, butter, almond meal,
confectioners' sugar and flour together in a bowl
with a hand whisk until combined. Pour into the
prepared pan, so that each cup is two-thirds full.

Place two or three raspberries on top of each friand
and bake for 25–30 minutes, or until a skewer
inserted in the center comes out clean. Leave them
in the pan for 5 minutes before tipping out onto
a cooling rack.

Dust the friands with confectioners' sugar and serve
warm. They're best eaten the day they're made.

CHOCOLATE-CHIP HOT CROSS BUNS

I have never been
a fan of raisins, currants or
candied fruits in sweets so I avoided
hot cross buns like the plague. After only
recently discovering that chocolate hot cross
buns existed, I developed a major obsession—
this is my take on the traditional recipe.

Keep in mind that you will need a piping bag
to pipe the crosses on top of the buns. If you
don't happen to have one at home, you can
make one easily by filling a zip-lock bag with
the paste and cutting a small hole
in one of the corners
of the bag. →

**" YOU ARE THE
CHOSEN BUN "**

MAKES 12

4 teaspoons dried yeast

1⅓ cups (330 ml) whole milk, warmed

⅓ cup (65 g) superfine sugar

5 cups (600 g) all-purpose flour, plus extra for dusting

1 teaspoon ground cinnamon

¼ cup (30 g) Dutch-processed cocoa powder, sifted

½ teaspoon sea salt

2¾ ounces (80 g) unsalted butter, chopped

1 large egg, lightly beaten

1¼ cups (200 g) dark chocolate chips

PASTE

¼ cup (35 g) all-purpose flour

2 teaspoons superfine sugar

¼ cup (60 ml) cold water

GLAZE

½ cup (100 g) superfine sugar

½ teaspoon vanilla bean paste

⅓ cup (100 ml) water

TIP: For an extra chocolate hit, serve warm with a dollop of Nutella. If you happen to have any leftovers, toast lightly and spread with butter.

Grease and line a 13 x 9 x 2½-inch (33 x 23 x 6 cm) baking pan with parchment paper.

Whisk the yeast with the milk and 1 tablespoon of the sugar in a small bowl until the yeast dissolves. Leave to stand in a warm place for 5 minutes, or until frothy.

Sift the flour, cinnamon, cocoa and salt into a large bowl, then rub the butter in with your fingertips to form a crumb. Stir in the remaining sugar, the frothy yeast mixture, egg and a little warm water (1 teaspoon at a time, if you feel it needs it) to make a soft dough. Cover the bowl with a dish towel and leave to stand in a warm place for an hour, or until the mixture has doubled in size.

Turn out the dough onto a floured surface. Knead for 8 minutes, then add the chocolate chips. Knead for a further 2 minutes, combining the chocolate chips, until the dough is smooth and elastic. Divide into 12 portions and roll each into a smooth ball. Place the balls on the prepared baking sheet in four rows of three, leaving a ½-inch (1.5 cm) gap between each to allow room for the dough to expand. Let stand in a warm place for 30 minutes, or until almost doubled in size.

Preheat the oven to 425°F (220°C.)

Make the flour paste for the crosses by sifting the flour and sugar into a small bowl. Gradually stir in enough of the water to make a smooth, thick paste. Transfer the paste to a piping bag fitted with a small plain nozzle (or use a zip-lock bag with the corner snipped off) and pipe crosses onto the buns.

Bake the buns for 20 minutes, or until they are golden-brown and sound hollow when tapped.

Meanwhile, to make the glaze, bring the sugar, vanilla and ⅓ cup (100 ml) of water to a boil, stirring until the sugar has dissolved.

Transfer the hot buns to a cooling rack and brush them with the hot glaze. Best eaten while still warm, or store in an airtight container at room temperature for up to 5 days and toast them to reheat.

TRIFLE WITH VANILLA MERINGUE SPONGE & MASCARPONE WHIPPED CREAM

Making a trifle can be a little time-consuming but, thankfully, the process can be spread out over a few days to make your life easier. The best thing about trifles is that they are so adaptable. I have used raspberry jello and red berries here as they are the most festive, but you can alter the recipe to include your favorite fillings and flavors. →

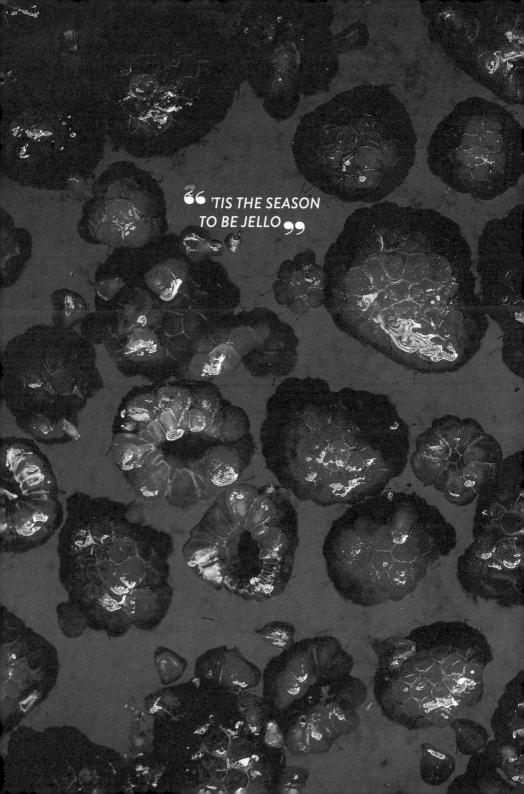

'TIS THE SEASON TO BE JELLO

SERVES 20

2 cups (250 g) fresh raspberries

edible gold dust, optional, to serve

JELL-O

2 x 3-ounce (85 g) packets raspberry gelatin

2 cups (480 ml) boiling water

1¾ cups (420 ml) cold water

2 cups (250 g) frozen raspberries

SPONGE CAKE

5½ ounces (150 g) unsalted butter, at room temperature

¾ cup (150 g) superfine sugar

1 teaspoon vanilla bean paste

2 large eggs, at room temperature, lightly beaten

1¼ cups (150 g) self-rising flour, sifted

½ teaspoon baking powder, sifted

¼ cup (60 ml) whole milk

MERINGUE

3 large egg whites, at room temperature

pinch of sea salt

¾ cup (150 g) superfine sugar

MASCARPONE WHIPPED CREAM

1 cup (250 g) mascarpone, at room temperature

¼ cup (50 g) superfine sugar

1 cup (250 ml) heavy whipping cream, at room temperature

1 teaspoon vanilla bean paste

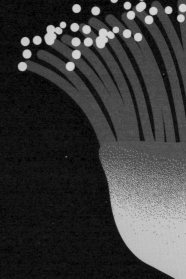

Rinse and dry your trifle serving bowl. I use a bowl that is 9 inches wide and 6½ inches high (23 x 17 cm). Whatever you use, it will need to fit a 9-inch/23-cm cake layer.

To make the gelatin, empty the contents of one packet of the gelatin into a bowl. Add 1 cup (250 ml) of the boiling water. Stir and dissolve well. Add ¾ cup (200 ml) of the cold water and stir. Pour the mixture into the trifle bowl and refrigerate until firm and wobbly, approximately 4 hours. Repeat with the second packet of gelatin, but once you have poured the gelatin mixture into the serving bowl, top with the frozen raspberries. Refrigerate until firm and wobbly.

While your gelatin sets, make your sponge. Preheat the oven to 350°F (170°C). Line a 9-inch (23 cm) springform pan with parchment paper.

Using a stand mixer fitted with the whisk attachment, cream the butter, sugar and vanilla on medium speed until pale and fluffy. Gradually add the eggs, beating well after each addition, until well combined.

Sift the dry ingredients into a bowl. Alternate between adding the dry ingredients and milk to the batter, folding with each addition. Pour the batter into the prepared pan and smooth the surface with the back of a spoon.

For the meringue, add the egg whites and salt into the clean, dry bowl of the stand mixer fitted with the whisk attachment and beat on medium speed until soft peaks form. Gradually add the sugar, beating until combined and the meringue is thick and glossy.

Spoon the meringue over the cake batter. Place the clean, dry pan in the oven and bake for 35–40 minutes. Set aside to cool in the pan.

To make the mascarpone whipped cream, beat the mascarpone and sugar in the stand mixer fitted with the whisk attachment until combined. Add the cream and vanilla and beat until stiff peaks form, about 3 minutes.

To assemble the trifle, remove the gelatin from the fridge. Delicately place the cake on top of the set gelatin. Spread the mascarpone whipped cream over the meringue. Top with the berries and a sprinkling of gold dust, if using, and serve immediately. Store leftovers covered in the fridge for up to 3 days.

APPLE
CRUMBLE

The simplicity of apple crumble is what first attracted me to making it. The fewer ingredients the better, and for a first-time baker (which I was at the time) it's a flawless recipe, too. It was the first dessert I ever made for my boyfriend at the time. I had him at the first mouthful, not only because of the combination of sugar and butter (which caramelizes in the oven) but also because everybody loves crumble and, frankly, our relationship would have been over if he didn't! →

SERVES 8

2 pounds (1 kg) Granny Smith
apples, peeled, cored and
thinly sliced

3 tablespoons (45 ml)
lemon juice

1 teaspoon ground cinnamon

ice cream, custard or heavy
whipping cream, to serve

TOPPING

9 ounces (250 g) unsalted butter

1¾ cups (225 g) all-purpose flour

1 cup (175 g) superfine sugar

pinch of ground nutmeg

1 cup (100 g) rolled oats

*"I APPLESOLUTELY
LOVE YOU"*

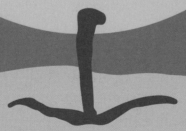

Preheat the oven to 350°F (180°C).

Combine the apple slices, lemon juice and cinnamon in a large bowl. Transfer to a 6-cup (1.5-liter) baking dish.

To make the topping, melt the butter in a small saucepan over medium heat. Place the flour, sugar, nutmeg and oats in a bowl. Pour the butter into the bowl and mix until combined.

Using your hands or a spoon, sprinkle the crumble topping evenly over the filling until your apples are covered. Bake for 40–45 minutes, or until the crumble is golden.

You can serve the crumble with ice cream, custard or cream. My go-to is vanilla bean whipped cream. For this I simply use 2 cups (480 ml) of heavy whipping cream and 1 teaspoon of vanilla bean paste. I whisk them in my stand mixer until soft peaks form and voilà!

The crumble is best eaten hot straight from the oven, but leftovers can be covered and stored in the fridge for up to 2 days.

TIP: You can split the ingredients and make two smaller crumbles if you like. I also like to make different combinations of fruit crumble, such as apple and pear, or strawberry and rhubarb.

LAYERED BERRY PAVLOVA

Each year, my bestie Gaby and I host an event called Friendsmas with some of our most favorite people. We spend the weekend cooking, and pavlova always makes an appearance as dessert. This is my recipe for a layered pavlova. If you only want to make a single pavlova shell, simply halve all of the ingredients but maintain the same temperature and cooking time.

You will know when you have soft peaks because the egg whites will look like white waves when you lift your whisk. Stiff peaks droop down and stick to the beater. It is imperative that you have your eggs at room temperature to achieve this.

Make sure that you only decorate your pavlova when you are ready to serve to avoid the meringue going soggy from the cream. It's a fun dessert to take to a friend's house as you can whip the cream and prepare the decorations in advance, then arrange it on-site. You can add any fruit you want, but I prefer red berries because they look so festive. You can also use blueberries, passionfruit, kiwi fruit or mango.

For me, this dish is almost a work of art. To give it that Klimt-esque midas touch, I use edible gold leaf and gold dust, which you can find at specialty stores or online. →

" I'M PAVLOVA
THE MOON "

SERVES 10

12 large egg whites,
at room temperature

4¼ cups (800 g)
superfine sugar

1¼ tablespoons corn starch

finely grated zest and juice
of 2 lemons

TOPPING

5 cups (1.2 liters) heavy
whipping cream

2 teaspoons vanilla bean paste

3¼ cups (500 g) fresh
strawberries, halved and tops
removed

¾ cup (125 g) fresh blueberries

edible gold dust, optional,
for decorating

2 cups (250 g) fresh raspberries

¾ cup (30 g) freeze-dried
raspberries, optional, for
decorating

edible flowers, optional,
for decorating

edible gold leaf, optional,
for decorating

Preheat the oven to 300°F (150°C). Line two baking sheets with parchment paper. Trace a circle on the underside of each sheet of parchment paper so that your pavlova shells are of equal size. (I trace around the inside of one of my 9-inch/ 23 cm springform cake pans, ensuring consistency every time!)

In the bowl of a stand mixer fitted with the whisk attachment, beat the egg whites until stiff peaks form. With the motor running, gradually add the sugar, one spoonful at a time, until you have a shiny and stiff meringue.

Add the corn starch, lemon zest and juice and fold the ingredients together using the paddle attachment.

Divide the meringue mixture evenly between the two baking sheets, spreading it gently to fill the circles. Place in the oven and cook for 1 hour. Remove from the oven and allow to cool completely.

For the topping, whip the cream and vanilla in the stand mixer fitted with the whisk attachment.

Place one of the pavlova shells on a platter (I usually pick whichever is the flatter of the two) and top with half the cream and a layer of strawberries. Place the second pavlova shell on top and repeat with the remaining cream and strawberries.

In a small bowl, cover your blueberries in gold dust (if using).

Add the blueberries and raspberries to the top of the pavlova so it appears full and abundant, and sprinkle with crumbled freeze-dried raspberries, if desired. If you are using them, add edible flowers and gold leaf to the top of your pavlova, too. The pavlova is best eaten immediately.

CAKES, BUNDTS & TARTS

PEAR &
ALMOND LOAF

This is
a show
stopper.
The stems
of the pears
are crucial to
this dessert.
I always poach
a few additional pears as
back up, in case any of their stems
break during the poaching process.
You will want to check the loaf at
the 20 minute mark and straighten
any pears that may have tilted to the
side to ensure you achieve this
picture-perfect result. →

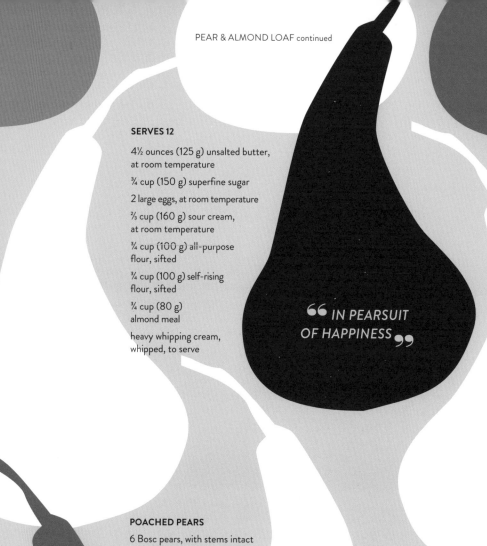

SERVES 12

4½ ounces (125 g) unsalted butter,
at room temperature

¾ cup (150 g) superfine sugar

2 large eggs, at room temperature

⅔ cup (160 g) sour cream,
at room temperature

¾ cup (100 g) all-purpose
flour, sifted

¾ cup (100 g) self-rising
flour, sifted

¾ cup (80 g)
almond meal

heavy whipping cream,
whipped, to serve

66 *IN PEARSUIT
OF HAPPINESS* 99

POACHED PEARS

6 Bosc pears, with stems intact

juice of 1 lemon

2 cups (400 g) superfine sugar

1 vanilla bean, split in two

Peel one pear at a time and sprinkle with lemon juice as you go to avoid browning. Place the sugar and 6 cups (1.5 litres) of water in a large saucepan over medium heat and simmer for 5 minutes, or until the sugar has dissolved. Add the pears and the vanilla pod halves. Cover the pears with a circle of parchment paper roughly the size of your sauce pan, with a small circle cut out of the center, and simmer for 15–20 minutes, or until tender. Turn occasionally to ensure even cooking. Set aside to cool in the liquid.

Preheat the oven to 325°F (160°C). Butter a 9 x 5 x 3-inch (23 x 13 x 7 cm) loaf pan and line the bottom and sides with parchment paper so it extends over the sides of the pan.

Using a stand mixer fitted with the paddle attachment, beat the butter and sugar until smooth. Add the eggs, one at a time, beating well after each addition. Add the sour cream and beat until combined. Fold in the sifted flours and almond meal.

Pour the batter into the prepared loaf pan. Strain the pears, then arrange three of them in a straight line down the center, with a 1-inch (3 cm) gap between each. Gently push the pears to the bottom of the pan.

Bake for 50 minutes, checking at the 20 minute mark to straighten any pears that may have tilted. Allow the loaf to cool completely in the pan, then carefully remove it by lifting the parchment paper and placing it on your serving plate, peeling off the paper. Serve with heavy whipping cream. Store leftovers in an airtight container in the fridge for 2–3 days.

TIPS: You can use the leftover pears for a second dessert served with ice cream, or for breakfast with muesli and Greek yogurt. You can poach the pears the day before and store them in their syrup until you're ready to bake.

CHOCOLATE BUTTERMILK CAKE

This recipe was first featured in an ebook I published and has since taken on a life of its own. It is a cake dedicated to the die-hard chocolate fans out there— a deliciously moist chocolate buttermilk cake slathered in an incredible chocolate cream cheese frosting. It's sweet and dark, and the buttermilk provides the perfect kiss of sourness to give you a balance of flavors that will fulfill the deepest desires of any chocolate lover. →

" IT DOESN'T GET BUTTER THAN THIS "

SERVES 8

2 cups (250 g) all-purpose
flour, sifted

1 teaspoon baking soda, sifted

1½ cups (300 g)
superfine sugar

4½ ounces (125 g) unsalted
butter, melted and cooled

⅓ cup (50 g) Dutch-processed
cocoa powder, sifted

1 large egg, at room temperature

½ cup (125 ml) buttermilk,
at room temperature

1 teaspoon vanilla extract

FROSTING

3½ ounces (100 g) unsalted
butter, at room temperature

⅓ cup (250 g) cream cheese,
at room temperature

¾ cup (100 g) confectioners'
sugar, sifted

⅓ cup (50 g) Dutch-processed
cocoa powder, sifted

Preheat the oven to 325°F (160°C). Grease and line a 9-inch (23 cm) springform pan.

Place the flour, baking soda and sugar in a bowl. Add the melted butter, cocoa and ⅔ cup (150 ml) of water and whisk to combine. Add the egg, buttermilk and vanilla and whisk to combine.

Pour the batter into the prepared pan.

Bake for 50–60 minutes, or until a skewer inserted in the center comes out clean. Leave to cool in the pan completely.

To make the frosting, place the butter and cream cheese in the bowl of a stand mixer fitted with the whisk attachment and beat until pale and creamy. Scrape down the side of the bowl, add the confectioners' sugar and cocoa and beat for a further 6–8 minutes, or until fluffy.

Spread the frosting over the cooled cake and serve. Store leftovers in an airtight container in the fridge for 2–3 days.

TIP: Try decorating this cake with chocolate-coated pretzels to give the cake a pop of salt and some crunch.

PRACTICE WHAT YOU PEACH

PEACH & RASPBERRY SHEET CAKE

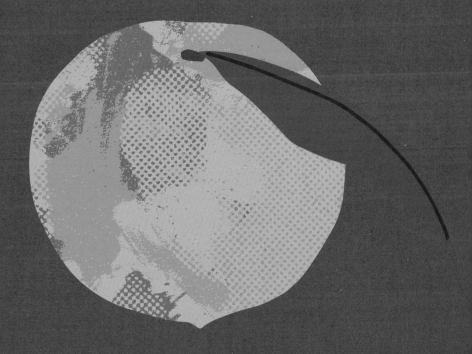

This is such an easy recipe and one that is my go-to if I have unexpected afternoon tea guests. It's fast, delicious, wonderfully vibrant and a recipe that you can bake all year round. Simply use canned sliced peaches and frozen raspberries if the fresh equivalents are out of season. You can, of course, swap out the peaches and raspberries for pears, blueberries or strawberries to create a delicious and warming afternoon treat. →

"YOU'VE GOT A PEACH OF MY HEART"

SERVES 15

1½ cups (185 g) self-rising flour

1 cup (170 g) superfine sugar

4½ ounces (125 g) unsalted butter, at room temperature

2 large eggs, at room temperature

⅓ cup (80 ml) whole milk

1½ teaspoons vanilla extract

4 yellow peaches, sliced into 1-inch (2 cm) wedges with skins on

1 cup (125 g) fresh raspberries

heavy whipping cream, whipped, to serve

Preheat the oven to 350°F (180°C). Grease a 13 x 9 x 2½-inch (33 x 23 x 6 cm) rectangular baking pan with nonstick cooking spray.

Place the flour, sugar, butter, eggs, milk and vanilla in the bowl of a stand mixer fitted with the whisk attachment. Beat on low speed until combined (this takes about 30 seconds). Increase the speed to high and beat for 2–3 minutes, or until thick and pale. Spoon the batter into the prepared pan and smooth the surface with the back of a spoon. The batter won't look like much at this stage, but don't worry—it rises beautifully in the oven. Arrange the peaches and raspberries on top of the batter, pressing down gently.

Bake for 30 minutes, or until golden and a skewer inserted in the center comes out clean.

I love to serve this warm, straight from the oven, with a generous dollop of cream. Store leftovers in an airtight container in the fridge for 2–3 days.

CAKES, BUNDTS & TARTS

MINI ESPRESSO CAKES

As a baker and dessert fiend who doesn't drink coffee, this is my ultimate labor of love. The combination of chocolate and coffee here is incredibly rich and satisfying. You want to use good-quality Dutch-processed cocoa powder to achieve the fudgiest result. Don't fret if, like me, you aren't a coffee drinker—the espresso merely enhances the flavor of the chocolate, and is perfectly complemented by the mascarpone frosting. →

MAKES 6

4 teaspoons instant
coffee granules

4 teaspoons (20 ml) boiling water

2 cups (250 g) all-purpose flour

½ cup (65 g) Dutch-processed
cocoa powder

1 tablespoon baking powder

1½ sticks (170 g) unsalted butter,
at room temperature

1¼ cups (225 g) light brown sugar

2 large eggs, at room temperature

1⅔ cups (400 ml) whole
milk, at room temperature

chocolate-coated coffee beans
or chocolate shavings, to serve

FROSTING

4 teaspoons instant
coffee granules

3 tablespoons (45 ml)
boiling water

4 cups (500 g)
confectioners' sugar

4 teaspoons Dutch-processed
cocoa powder

1 cup (250 g) mascarpone,
at room temperature

Preheat the oven to 325°F (160°C). Grease a 13 x 9 x 2½-inch (33 x 23 x 6 cm) rectangular baking pan and line the base with parchment paper.

Dissolve the coffee granules in boiling water and set aside to cool.

Sift the flour, cocoa powder and baking powder into a bowl.

In a stand mixer fitted with the whisk attachment, beat the butter and sugar until pale and fluffy, scraping down the side of the bowl throughout. Add the eggs and beat until combined. Add the coffee and mix, then alternately add the milk and dry ingredients and beat until just combined.

Spoon the batter into the prepared pan. Bake for 50 minutes, or until a skewer inserted in the center comes out clean. Cool the cake in its pan on a cooling rack, then, using a 3½-inch (9 cm) round cookie cutter, cut out six mini cakes.

For the frosting, dissolve the coffee in the boiling water and allow to cool. Sift the confectioners' sugar and cocoa powder together into a medium bowl. Add the coffee and mascarpone and whisk until smooth. Spread the frosting over the cooled cakes and scatter with the chocolate-coated coffee beans or chocolate shavings. Store leftovers in an airtight container at room temperature for up to 2 days.

TIP: Alternatively, leave the cake whole to serve 15.

LEMON OLIVE OIL CAKE

It seems that more and more of my friends are becoming gluten or dairy intolerant. Thankfully, this recipe comes to the rescue when celebrating with them. Baking with olive oil brings an incredible moistness you don't seem to get with butter. →

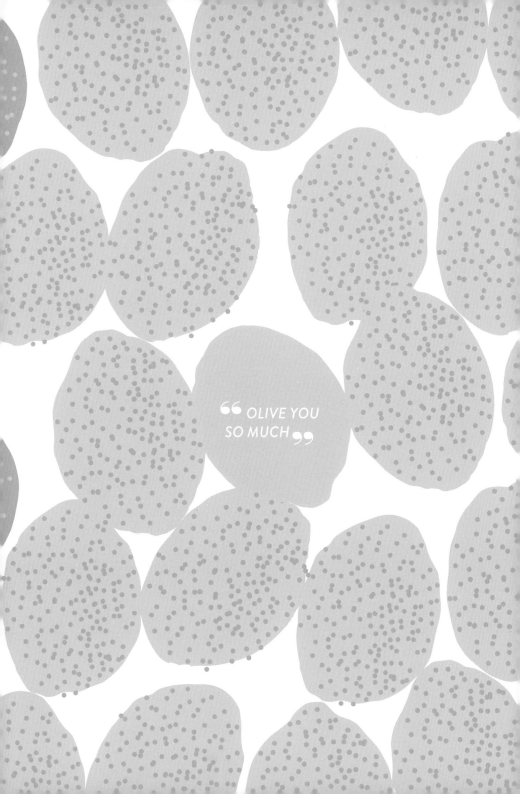

" OLIVE YOU
SO MUCH "

SERVES 12

1⅓ cups (150 g) hazelnut meal

½ teaspoon baking soda, sifted

finely grated zest of 1 lemon, plus extra to serve

pinch of sea salt

⅔ cup ounces (150 ml) extra-virgin olive oil

1 cup (200 g) superfine sugar

3 large eggs, at room temperature

2 teaspoons vanilla extract

confectioners' sugar, sifted, for dusting

crème fraîche, to serve

Preheat the oven to 350°F (170°C). Grease an 8-inch (20 cm) springform pan with olive oil and line the base with parchment paper.

In a small bowl, combine the hazelnut meal, baking soda, lemon zest and sea salt.

Place the olive oil, superfine sugar and eggs in a large bowl and beat with a hand-held electric mixer on high speed for 3 minutes, or until the mixture is pale and resembles heavy whipping cream.

Reduce the speed to medium–low and add the vanilla, beating continuously. Once combined, add the hazelnut mixture and stir gently with a spatula.

Pour the batter into the prepared pan and bake for 40–45 minutes.

Cool in the pan for 10 minutes on a cooling rack, then remove the cake from the pan and set aside to cool.

Dust with confectioners' sugar and sprinkle with a little extra lemon zest, then serve with crème fraîche. Store leftovers in an airtight container at room temperature for 2–3 days.

TIP: *To glam things up, try using a vegetable peeler to peel long, thick strips of zest from another lemon. Thinly slice the strips, place them in 2 tablespoons of superfine sugar and rub in with your fingertips until combined. Place on top of the cake to decorate.*

VANILLA CAKE WITH RICOTTA FROSTING & ROASTED PEACHES

This is a simple cake, so you want to ensure you are baking with good-quality ingredients to allow the flavors to shine. Buy the best-quality ricotta, eggs and peaches you can get your hands on. The peaches in particular are the hero of this dish. They make my mouth water and, when roasted, their fragrance is all consuming. →

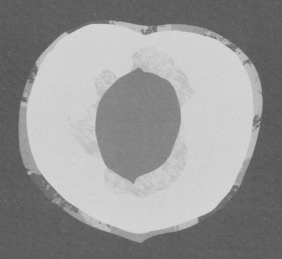

SERVES 8

1½ cups (185 g)
self-rising flour

1 cup (170 g) superfine sugar

4½ ounces (125 g) unsalted
butter, at room temperature

2 large eggs, at room temperature

⅓ cup (80 ml) whole milk

1½ teaspoons vanilla extract

edible flowers, optional,
for decorating

ROASTED PEACHES

3 peaches, halved

4 teaspoons (20 ml) honey

1 vanilla bean, split

FROSTING

1 cup (250 g) full-fat ricotta,
at room temperature

1 cup (250 ml) heavy whipping
cream, at room temperature

¾ cup (100 g) confectioners'
sugar, sifted

Preheat the oven to 350°F (180°C). Grease an 8-inch (20 cm) springform pan and line the base with parchment paper.

Place the flour, sugar, butter, eggs, milk and vanilla in the bowl of a stand mixer fitted with the whisk attachment. Beat on low speed until combined (about 30 seconds). Increase the speed to high and beat for 2–3 minutes, or until thick and pale. Spoon the batter into the prepared pan.

Bake for 45 minutes, or until a skewer inserted in the center comes out clean. Leave to cool in the pan for 5 minutes before turning out onto a cooling rack to cool completely.

To make the roasted peaches, arrange the peaches cut-side up on a baking sheet sprayed with nonstick cooking spray. Drizzle with 1 tablespoon of water and the honey, then scrape the seeds from the vanilla bean over top. Add the empty vanilla bean pod to the baking sheet. Bake for 30 minutes, or until soft. Remove from the oven and leave to cool completely.

Once the cake and peaches have cooled, prepare the frosting. Beat the ricotta, cream and confectioners' sugar until thickened and combined.

Spread the frosting over the top of the cake. Just before serving, arrange the roasted peaches over the frosting and drizzle any additional peach syrup over the top. Finish with some edible flowers, if you like. This cake is best eaten on the day it is made.

"JUMP ON THE
BUNDTWAGON"

BROWN BUTTER BUNDT CAKE

This cake is a perfect example of how a simple classic can inspire anyone to bake. The brown butter is really the hero of this dish, so it's imperative you get the butter as brown as can be without burning it. This can be achieved by using a high heat on the stove and then physically removing the pan from the heat as it bubbles. Keep repeating this until you have a golden-brown color. The residual heat in the pan will darken the butter even as you take it off the stove, so make sure you keep an eye on this as you want brown butter, not burnt! →

SERVES 12

6½ ounces (185 g) unsalted butter

2⅔ cups (335 g) all-purpose flour, sifted

1½ teaspoons baking powder, sifted

1¼ cups (210 g) superfine sugar

4 large eggs, at room temperature

2 teaspoons vanilla extract

¾ cup (180 ml) buttermilk

confectioners' sugar, sifted, for dusting

Preheat the oven to 325°F (160°C). Generously grease a classic-sized Bundt pan with butter and flour, or use nonstick cooking spray.

Melt the butter in a small saucepan over medium heat until foamy and turning amber in color, stirring occasionally. Ensure that you keep an eye on the pan as it only takes a few seconds to burn the butter. Once browned, pour the butter (including the brown specks at the bottom of the pan, which are the milk solids that have separated) into a small bowl and set aside to cool.

Whisk together the flour and baking powder in a small bowl.

Pour the browned butter and sugar into the bowl of a stand mixer fitted with the whisk attachment and beat until pale. Add the eggs, one at a time, beating well after each addition. Add the vanilla and buttermilk and beat until just combined. Reduce the speed to low, add the dry ingredients and beat until just combined. Pour the batter into the Bundt pan.

Bake for 1 hour, or until a skewer inserted in the cake comes out clean. Allow to cool completely in the pan, then turn out onto a serving dish, dust with confectioners' sugar and serve. Store leftovers in an airtight container at room temperature for 2–3 days.

TIP: *You can also make this cake in a 9 x 5 x 3-inch (23 x 13 x 7 cm) loaf pan.*

TIRAMISU
SWISS ROLL

This recipe combines two desserts in one, with an incredible tiramisu filling wrapped inside a moist sponge cake. It is an impressive way to celebrate any occasion. →

"WAKE ME UP BEFORE YOU COCOA"

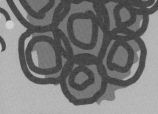

SERVES 8

3 large eggs, at room temperature

⅔ cup (125 g) superfine sugar

⅔ cup (80 g) all-purpose flour, sifted

½ teaspoon baking powder, sifted

¼ cup (30 g) Dutch-processed cocoa powder, sifted, plus extra to dust dish towel

1 tablespoon confectioners' sugar, sifted, to dust dish towel

4 teaspoons instant coffee granules

⅓ cup (100 ml) boiling water

4 teaspoons Frangelico

½ cup (80 g) dark chocolate (70% cocoa), roughly chopped

FILLING

2 cups (500 g) mascarpone, at room temperature

¾ cup (200 ml) heavy whipping cream, at room temperature

¼ cup (60 g) confectioners' sugar, sifted

1 teaspoon vanilla bean paste

TOPPING

leftover filling mixture

2 tablespoons plus 1½ teaspoons Dutch-processed cocoa powder, sifted

gourmet dark chocolate bar, refrigerated, for curls

First, make the filling by placing the mascarpone in the bowl of a stand mixer fitted with the whisk attachment and beating until smooth. Add the cream, confectioners' sugar and vanilla and whisk until creamy and smooth. Place in the fridge, covered in plastic wrap, until ready to use.

Preheat the oven to 350°F (180°C). Grease a 15 x 10 x 1-inch (38 x 25 x 3 cm) jelly roll pan with nonstick cooking spray and line with parchment paper.

Whisk the eggs and sugar in the bowl of the stand mixer on high until thick and pale and the mixture has doubled in size (about 4–6 minutes). Sift the flour, baking and cocoa powders once more over the egg mixture. Use a metal spoon to fold the mixture until combined, maintaining as much air as possible. Pour into the prepared pan and gently smooth the surface with the back of a spoon. Bake for 10–12 minutes, or until the sponge springs back slightly when touched.

While the cake is in the oven, lay a clean dish towel on your kitchen counter and dust with the extra cocoa powder and confectioners' sugar. Remove the cake from the oven and turn out the sponge onto the prepared dish towel. Peel the parchment paper off gently. Starting at the short edge, tightly roll the cake in the towel and leave to cool completely.

Dissolve the coffee granules in the boiling water, then add the Frangelico and set aside to cool.

Unroll the cooled cake. Using a pastry brush, brush the coffee mixture over the cake until covered and all the coffee has been used. Spread the mascarpone mixture over the sponge, leaving a ½-inch (1 cm) border to allow for spreading. Sprinkle with chopped dark chocolate. Gently roll the cake back into a log shape and place on plastic wrap, wrapping the cake and sealing both ends. Place in the fridge to set, alongside a small bowl of any leftover filling mixture.

To serve, remove the cake from the fridge and plastic wrap and spread the remaining filling mixture over the top until smooth. Dust with cocoa powder and decorate with chocolate curls. Store leftovers, covered, in the fridge for up to 2 days.

APPLE TEA CAKE

This cake is completely uncomplicated, and you'll please
everyone in the room by allowing the simplest ingredients
to play hero. I bake with Granny Smith apples as they
hold their shape incredibly well. →

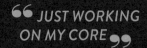

*JUST WORKING
ON MY CORE*

SERVES 12

7 ounces (200 g) unsalted butter, at room temperature

1 cup (175 g) superfine sugar

1 teaspoon vanilla bean paste

3 large eggs, at room temperature

1¾ cup (225 g) self-rising flour, sifted

½ cup (125 ml) whole milk

3 small Granny Smith apples, peeled, cored and halved

turbinado sugar, for sprinkling

Preheat the oven to 325°F (160°C). Grease and line the base of a 9-inch (23 cm) springform pan with parchment paper.

Beat the butter, superfine sugar and vanilla in the bowl of a stand mixer fitted with the whisk attachment until light and fluffy. Add the eggs one at a time, making sure to beat well after each addition. Add the flour and milk and beat to combine. Pour the batter into the prepared pan.

Cut thin, deep slits into the uncut, round side of each apple half. Arrange the apples cut-side down, and gently push them into the batter. Sprinkle the turbinado sugar over the apples.

Bake for 1 hour, or until golden and a skewer inserted in the center of the cake comes out clean. Leave to cool in the pan for 15 minutes before turning out onto a cooling rack to cool completely. Store leftovers in an airtight container at room temperature for 2–3 days.

CHOCOLATE & ROSEMARY BUNDT CAKE

Feeling festive? Then this is the cake you must bake. I love using sprigs of rosemary as little Christmas trees. Simply trim the sprigs and place them on top of the cake. You can dust with confectioners' sugar to make it look like a sprinkling of snow. →

SERVES 12

2 cups (250 g) all-purpose flour

½ cup (65 g) Dutch-processed cocoa powder

1 tablespoon baking powder

1 tablespoon finely diced rosemary leaves

2 sticks (170 g) unsalted butter, at room temperature

1¼ cups (225 g) light brown sugar

2 large eggs, at room temperature

1⅔ cups (400 ml) whole milk

TOPPING

6 rosemary sprigs, of different heights

confectioners' sugar, sifted, for dusting

heavy whipping cream, whipped, to serve

Preheat the oven to 325°F (160°C). Grease a classic-sized Bundt pan generously with butter and flour or nonstick cooking spray.

Sift the flour, cocoa powder and baking powder into a bowl, then stir through the rosemary. In a stand mixer fitted with the whisk attachment, beat the butter and sugar until pale and fluffy. Add the eggs and beat until combined. Alternately add the milk and dry ingredients to the butter mixture, then spoon the batter into the prepared pan.

Bake for 50 minutes, or until a skewer inserted in the cake comes out clean. Cool in the pan on a cooling rack.

Once the cake has cooled, remove it from the pan and place on your chosen platter. Decorate with the rosemary sprigs and dust with confectioners' sugar. Serve with a dollop of cream. Store leftovers in an airtight container at room temperature for 2–3 days.

" EAT, DRINK
AND BE
ROSEMARY "

SEASONAL FRUIT
RICOTTA TART

A crunchy cocoa cookie base and creamy chocolate ricotta filling make
this tart a chocolate lover's dream. Think of this as a delicious Italian
cheesecake and, given that the ricotta is the queen here, you will want
to buy the best quality that you can afford. You can decorate the top of
the tart with any fruit that is in season. Here, I have used fresh figs,
Muscat grapes and candied orange slices. →

SERVES 12

1 package (400 g) digestive cookies

½ cup (50 g) Dutch-processed cocoa powder, sifted

5½ ounces (150 g) unsalted butter, at room temperature

1 teaspoon sea salt

FILLING

3 sheets titanium-strength (120 bloom) unflavored gelatin

2¾ cups (650 g) full-fat ricotta, at room temperature

1½ cups (350 g) mascarpone, at room temperature

2 cups (250 g) confectioners' sugar, sifted

¼ cup (30 g) Dutch-processed cocoa powder, sifted

4 teaspoons instant coffee granules

¾ cup (200 ml) heavy whipping cream, whipped to soft peaks

TOPPING

seasonal fruit of your choice

Preheat the oven to 350°F (170°C). Grease a 9-inch (23 cm) springform pan and line the base with baking paper.

Process the cookies in a food processor until finely ground or, alternatively, place them in a zip-lock bag and beat with a rolling pin. Add the cocoa powder, butter and salt and process to combine. Press evenly into the base of the prepared pan. Bake for 15 minutes, then allow to cool.

To make the filling, soak the gelatin sheets in a bowl of cold water until soft (approximately 5 minutes), then gently wring out any excess water.

Beat the ricotta, mascarpone, confectioners' sugar and cocoa powder in a stand mixer fitted with the whisk attachment until smooth. Bring ½ cup (100 ml) of water to a boil and pour it into a small heatproof bowl, then add the gelatin and coffee granules and stir until dissolved. Leave to cool, then add it to the ricotta mixture and beat until combined. Fold in the whipped cream.

Spread the filling evenly over the base, smoothing the top with the back of a spatula. Refrigerate for at least 8 hours, or preferably overnight, until set.

To serve, remove the tart from the fridge and top with seasonal fruit of your choice. Store covered in the fridge for up to 2 days.

NEAPOLITAN
MARBLE CAKE

Marble cakes are one of my favorite types of cake.
As a child, I was always intrigued by the way the different
colored batters blended together. (I still am!) To create
a marbled effect, dollop each of the colored batters into the
cake pan, then pull a skewer back and forth through the mixture
to incorporate each color. Be careful not to over-mix,
though, or the colors won't be as defined.

If you like, make six mini Bundts instead of one
Bundt loaf (see page 7). →

**" YOU ARE
BATTER THAN ALL
OF THE FLAVORS
COMBINED "**

SERVES 12

4½ ounces (120 g) unsalted butter, at room temperature

1¼ cups (220 g) superfine sugar

2 large eggs, at room temperature

2⅓ cups (300 g) self-rising flour

⅔ cup (150 ml) whole milk

rose pink food coloring

1 teaspoon strawberry essence

2½ tablespoons Dutch-processed cocoa powder, sifted

1 teaspoon vanilla bean paste

shredded coconut, for decorating

GANACHE

2 cups (250 g) Ruby Chocolate Callebaut callets (small discs, see Tip)

4 teaspoons softened butter

Preheat the oven to 325°F (160°C). Grease a 9 x 5 x 3-inch (23 x 13 x 7 cm) loaf pan or 12 x 6 x 3-inch (30 x 15.5 x 7.5 cm) Bundt loaf pan with nonstick cooking spray.

Using a stand mixer fitted with the whisk attachment, beat the butter and sugar until creamy. Add the eggs and beat lightly to combine. Alternately add half of the flour and milk, then repeat and beat until just combined.

Divide the batter among three small bowls. To one, add a few drops of pink food coloring and the strawberry essence. To another, mix in the sifted cocoa powder. To the third, add the vanilla.

Using a tablespoon of batter at a time, spoon the batter into the prepared pan, alternating among the three colors. Use a skewer to marble the batter, then bake for 30 minutes, or until a skewer inserted in the center comes out clean. Leave to cool in the pan for 5 minutes before transferring to a cooling rack to cool completely.

To make the ganache, melt the chocolate callets in a double boiler, or in a heatproof bowl set over a saucepan of simmering water (ensuring the bowl doesn't touch the water). Add the butter and stir to create a wetter, silkier ganache.

Turn the cake out of the pan onto a serving plate. Pour the ganache over the cooled cake and top with shredded coconut. Store leftovers in an airtight container at room temperature for 2–3 days.

TIP: If you can't get your hands on Ruby Chocolate, which can be found at specialty stores or online, simply make a milk, dark or white chocolate ganache instead.

VANILLA CHIFFON CAKE

This recipe combines two of my great loves—pavlova and cake—to create a dessert that is ridiculously light and fluffy. For this recipe, you will need an angel food cake pan (ideally with a removable base and feet) to give the cake its incredible shape.

The main point of difference with this recipe compared to others in my book is that you must leave your baking pan ungreased. As this cake rises, its batter is able to cling to the pan, giving it an incredibly fluffy texture and height. →

I CAN'T CAKE MY EYES OFF YOU

SERVES 12

12 large egg whites,
at room temperature

1 teaspoon cream of tartar

1½ cups (275 g)
superfine sugar

2 teaspoons vanilla extract

1¼ cups (150 g)
all-purpose flour

5 cups (1.2 liters) heavy
whipping cream

1 teaspoon vanilla bean paste

3⅓ cups (500 g)
strawberries, halved
and tops removed

sifted confectioners' sugar,
for dusting

*TIP: Because of the height
of this cake, you may find
the top browns too quickly.
If this is the case, simply
cover the cake pan with
heavy-duty aluminum foil to
prevent the top from burning.*

Preheat the oven to 350°F (180°C). Do not grease your angel food cake pan!

In the bowl of a stand mixer fitted with the whisk attachment, whisk the egg whites and the cream of tartar on medium speed until soft peaks form. Gradually (and patiently) add the sugar, one spoonful at a time, and beat until stiff peaks form, just like a pavlova base. Whisk in the vanilla.

Remove the bowl from the stand mixer. Sift one-third of the flour over the egg white mixture, then fold the ingredients together with a metal spoon. Repeat with the remaining flour until fully incorporated.

Scrape half of the batter into the ungreased angel food cake pan. Using a metal spoon or spatula, smooth the batter evenly throughout the pan. Scrape the remaining batter into the pan, spreading evenly and gently smoothing the top with the back of the metal spoon.

Bake for 35–40 minutes, or until the top is puffed, lightly golden and springs back when touched.

Turn the cake upside-down immediately after pulling it out of the oven, and leave it to cool on a cooling rack (or, if your pan has feet, simply rest upside-down on those). Once completely cool, gently shake the pan and run a knife around the edge to release the cake. Cut the cake in half horizontally and place the bottom half on your desired serving plate.

In the bowl of a stand mixer fitted with the whisk attachment, whip the cream and vanilla until stiff peaks form, though be careful not to over-whip. If you do happen to over-whip your cream, gently whisk in a few additional teaspoons of heavy whipping cream and the mixture will balance out again. Cover the bottom half of the cake with a layer of whipped cream and strawberry halves. Place the second layer of cake on top and ice with the remaining whipped cream. To serve, top the cake with the remaining strawberries and dust with confectioners' sugar. Store leftovers covered in the fridge for up to 2 days.

LEMON CAKE WITH RASPBERRY BUTTERCREAM

This is the cake you'll make once you feel confident about your baking and you also want to show that you're not too shabby on the frosting. It's actually dead easy, and there is a sneaky trick I want to highlight here. When frosting the cake, use a lazy Susan. It helps you to keep the spatula steady and gives the cake a nice, even finish (it doesn't have to be perfect; in fact I prefer a more rustic look, but the spinning makes it so much easier to even out the frosting). You can also add more raspberries to your buttercream, depending on the color and consistency you would like. →

"TOO HARD TO REZEST"

SERVES 12

9 ounces (250 g) unsalted
butter, at room temperature

2 cups (360 g) superfine sugar

2 teaspoons vanilla bean paste

4 large eggs, at room
temperature

1 cup (250 ml) buttermilk

finely grated zest and juice
of 2 lemons

6 cups (750 g) self-rising flour

3¼ cups (70 g) freeze-dried
raspberries

RASPBERRY BUTTERCREAM

2 cups (250 g) fresh raspberries

2 teaspoons lemon juice

2½ tablespoons (40 ml)
superfine sugar

12½ ounces (350 g) unsalted
butter, at room temperature

2 teaspoons vanilla bean paste

4 cups (500 g) confectioners'
sugar, sifted

FILLING

1⅔ cups (400 g) full-fat ricotta,
at room temperature

1⅔ cups (400 g) mascarpone,
at room temperature

5 cups (1.2 liters) heavy
whipping cream, plus ¼ cup
(60 ml) extra

4 teaspoons vanilla bean paste

2 cups (250 g) fresh raspberries

TIP: *For perfectly
even layers, weigh your
batter-filled cake pans
before baking.*

Preheat the oven to 350°F (180°C). Grease and line two 9-inch (23 cm) springform pans with parchment paper.

Place the butter, superfine sugar and vanilla in the bowl of a stand mixer fitted with the whisk attachment and beat until light and creamy. Add the eggs and beat well. Add the milk, lemon zest and juice and flour and mix to combine.

Divide the batter between the prepared baking pans and smooth with a spatula. Bake for 40 minutes, or until a skewer inserted in the center comes out clean, swapping the cakes halfway through to ensure even baking. Set the baking pans on cooling racks and leave to cool.

To make the buttercream, puree the raspberries, lemon juice and superfine sugar in the bowl of a food processor until smooth. Pass the mixture through a fine sieve into a bowl, pressing on the solids to extract as much liquid as possible.

In the bowl of a stand mixer fitted with the whisk attachment, beat the butter and vanilla on high speed until pale and fluffy. Reduce the speed to medium and add the confectioners' sugar in three batches, beating well after each addition and scraping down the side of the bowl as needed. Add the berry puree and beat until combined. Set aside.

For the filling, process the ricotta and mascarpone in a food processor until smooth. Whip the heavy cream and vanilla in the bowl of the stand mixer fitted with the whisk attachment. Add the ricotta mixture and the extra ¼ cup heavy cream and beat until combined.

To construct the cake, cut each cooled cake in half horizontally, trimming the top of each cake to create four flat, even layers. Place the base of one cake on a serving platter over your lazy Susan. Top the base with one-third of the filling and a sprinkling of fresh raspberries. Repeat with two more layers and the remaining whipped cream and raspberries, then place the final cake half on top.

To ice the cake, dollop a large spoonful of buttercream onto the cake and smooth it with a palette knife. Spread the frosting around the side of the cake and smooth with the palette knife.

Finish by decorating with the freeze-dried raspberries. You can add a splash of color by placing fresh flowers on top as we have done here—but please note that these are not edible. Store leftovers covered in the fridge for up to 2 days.

CHOCOLATE GANACHE & BLACKBERRY BUNDT CAKE

A reminder that you will need a special cake pan called a Bundt pan to create this mesmerising shape. If you don't have one, you can bake this cake in an 8-inch (20 cm) springform pan, though it won't be as visually striking. As with all Bundt cakes, you need to grease your pan generously with a nonstick cooking spray, such as canola oil. Most importantly though, you want to allow your cake to cool completely in the pan before removing. →

“ YOU'RE THE ONE THAT I BUNDT ”

SERVES 12

2 cups (250 g) all-purpose flour

½ cup (65 g) Dutch-processed cocoa powder

1 tablespoon baking powder

1½ sticks (170 g) unsalted butter, at room temperature

1¼ cups (225 g) light brown sugar

2 large eggs, at room temperature

1⅔ cups (400 ml) whole milk

2 cups (250 g) fresh blackberries or berries of your choice

CHOCOLATE GANACHE

⅔ cups (150 ml) heavy whipping cream

1 cup (150 g) dark chocolate (70% cocoa), roughly chopped

Preheat the oven to 325°F (160°C). Generously spray a classic-sized Bundt pan with nonstick cooking spray.

Sift the flour, cocoa powder and baking powder into a bowl.

In a stand mixer fitted with the whisk attachment, beat the butter and sugar until pale and fluffy. Add the eggs and beat until combined. Alternately add the milk and dry ingredients and mix until combined. Spoon the batter into the prepared pan.

Bake for 50 minutes, or until a skewer inserted in the cake comes out clean. Cool in its pan on a cooling rack. (Warning: do not attempt to remove the cake from the pan until it has cooled completely, or you might end up with a hot mess.)

Once the cake has cooled, make the ganache. Heat the cream in a small saucepan until it begins to simmer. Remove from the heat and add the chocolate. Leave it to melt for 2–3 minutes, then whisk until smooth.

Carefully remove the cake from the pan and place it on a platter. Pour the ganache over the cake and let it run down the sides, following the shape of the Bundt.

Arrange the blackberries on top of the cake and serve. Store leftovers in an airtight container at room temperature for 2–3 days.

CONVERSION CHARTS

"MY RULE OF CRUMB"

Measuring cups and spoons may vary slightly from one country to another, but the difference is generally not enough to affect a recipe. All cup and spoon measures are level.

One standard US measuring cup holds 8 fluid ounces (240 ml). One standard teaspoon holds holds ½ fluid ounce (5 ml). North America, New Zealand and the UK use a 15 ml (3-teaspoon) tablespoon, while Australia uses a 20 ml (4-teaspoon) tablespoon.

OVEN TEMPERATURES

CELSIUS	FAHRENHEIT
100°C	200°F
120°C	250°F
150°C	300°F
160°C	325°F
180°C	350°F
200°C	400°F
220°C	425°F

FAHRENHEIT	GAS MARK
250°F	½
275°F	1
300°F	2
325°F	3
350°F	4
375°F	5
400°F	6
425°F	7

DRY MEASURES

The most accurate way to measure dry ingredients is to weigh them. However, if using a cup, add the ingredient loosely to the cup and level with a knife; don't compact the ingredient unless the recipe requests 'firmly packed'.

LIQUID MEASURES

ONE AMERICAN PINT	ONE IMPERIAL PINT
16 fl oz (500 ml)	20 fl oz (600 ml)

CUP	METRIC	IMPERIAL
⅛ cup	30 ml	1 fl oz
¼ cup	60 ml	2 fl oz
⅓ cup	80 ml	2½ fl oz
½ cup	120 ml	4 fl oz
⅔ cup	160 ml	5½ fl oz
¾ cup	180 ml	6 fl oz
1 cup	240 ml	8 fl oz
2 cups	480 ml	16 fl oz
2¼ cups	540 ml	18 fl oz
4 cups	1 litre	32 fl oz

LENGTH

METRIC	IMPERIAL
3 mm	⅛ inch
6 mm	¼ inch
1 cm	½ inch
2.5 cm	1 inch
5 cm	2 inches
18 cm	7 inches
20 cm	8 inches
23 cm	9 inches
25 cm	10 inches
30 cm	12 inches

METRIC	IMPERIAL
15 g	½ oz
30 g	1 oz
60 g	2 oz
125 g	4 oz (¼ lb)
185 g	6 oz
250 g	8 oz (½ lb)
375 g	12 oz (¾ lb)
500 g	16 oz (1 lb)
1 kg	32 oz (2 lb)

THANKS A BUNDTCH

❝ *YOU ARE THE ICING ON MY CAKE* **❞**

A heartfelt thanks to everyone at Running Press for making my dreams come true by bringing this "little book that could" to the USA.

My thanks, especially, to the editorial team for their insight, patience, and guidance in converting these recipes and perfecting my Australian-isms for a new market. Thank you to my incredible editors Britny Brooks-Perilli, Kristen Wiewora, and Martine Lleonart, to my designer Frances Soo Ping Chow, as well as the wonderful marketing, publicity, and sales teams that have championed this little book.

Of course, I owe it all to the delightful Dan Lazar. Who would have thought a chance meeting at an event in Sydney, and a shared love of dessert, would lead to an introduction with the sensational Susan Ginsburg? Susan, thank you for your belief in me and for loving this book as much as I do. I am so grateful to you and Catherine Bradshaw for all your support and encouragement.

And, finally, my thanks goes to each and every one of you. Thank you for buying this little book and thank you for baking. I hope it brings as much joy and happiness into your lives as it has into mine.

INDEX

**GOOD THINGS COME
TO THOSE WHO BAKE**

Running Press
Hachette Book Group
1290 Avenue of the Americas, New York, NY 10104
www.runningpress.com
@Running_Press

Printed in China

Originally published in 2019 by Pan Macmillan in Australia
First U.S. Edition: March 2021

Published by Running Press, an imprint of Perseus Books, LLC, a subsidiary of Hachette Book Group, Inc. The Running Press name and logo is a trademark of the Hachette Book Group.

The Hachette Speakers Bureau provides a wide range of authors for speaking events. To find out more, go to www.hachettespeakersbureau.com or call (866) 376-6591.

The publisher is not responsible for websites (or their content) that are not owned by the publisher.

Edited by Martine Lleonart
Index by Helena Holmgren
Prop and food styling by Lee Blaylock
Food preparation by Amelia Brown, Charlotte Ree,
   Diego Vidal, and Emma Warren.
Typeset by Megan Ellis

Library of Congress Control Number: 2020948462

ISBNs: 978-0-7624-7331-1 (hardcover),
978-0-7624-7332-8 (ebook)

1010

10 9 8 7 6 5 4 3 2 1